"Good Morning World!"

A Beginner's Guide To Starting Your Own Internet Radio Station

Chris Bechervaise

© 2012 Chris Bechervaise

All rights reserved

ISBN 978-1-291-06642-5

Contents

Introduction	4
Before you start	5
Equipment	12
Servers	17
Imaging – sounding and looking professional	21
Rigging for live broadcast	23
Starting a live broadcast	29
Recording a broadcast	33
Pre-recorded shows	36
Pictures of equipment	38
Recommended resources	48

Introduction

Whether you want to start a radio station to promote a local club or society, to promote your business, or just "wanna be a DJ", the internet is increasingly becoming a powerful tool for broadcasting all over the World. More and more home entertainment systems and mobile phones are including the facility to "tune-in" to internet radio stations, and there are at the time of going to print, over 50,000 stations broadcasting at any one time, with representatives from every nation. Indeed, it is the opinion of some that the days of airwave radio are numbered.

Using jargon-free language where possible, this publication aims to provide those with no previous experience of the broadcasting industry with a guide to setting-up and getting on air. We will look at the equipment needed, software, legalities, servers, getting on air and pre-recording shows for broadcast.

Before you start

So, you've decided you'll definitely start a radio station and start dreaming of presenting your own show to a worldwide audience. Well, that's all fine, but before you go out and buy that microphone you've always wanted, make yourself a coffee, grab a piece of blank paper and a pen and sit down. One of the biggest mistakes new internet radio station owners make (including myself) is thinking about the end product without considering how they are going to get there and things to take into consideration! So a little planning is required, and there are a number of questions which need to be answered:

What type of shows will I be broadcasting?

You may well already have a good idea about what you want to do, but this may affect the equipment you need. For example, my own radio station broadcasts live football (soccer) commentaries and magazine shows. When we're not broadcasting live, we broadcast pre-recorded mixed music shows 24/7. Because we do many live outside broadcasts (outside the studio), we still have to ensure that we have access to the internet via a broadband service. This therefore entails the need for various additional forms of equipment, not least a mobile broadband dongle to allow us to broadcast via the internet when out and about at locations where free wireless or wired broadband isn't provided.

How long will the shows be?

If you're going to be a "one-person band" then I guess it doesn't really matter how long your shows are – it's up to you. But if you have other people doing shows you may wish to consider the length of the shows. As most small internet radio stations are run by unpaid volunteers, you may find that if others are asked to commit to even one two-hour show every month, they may lose their enthusiasm after a few months. One way of counteracting this is by giving regular feedback about their show quality and listener stats, another way is of course to pay your presenters!

How often will I be broadcasting?

One thing you will need to decide is how often your service will be on air and for how long. There may be a number of factors which may influence this decision.

Firstly, your own time commitment and the commitment of others. So many small internet radio stations find themselves unable to meet their broadcast pledges because they try to run before they can walk. If you are only able to broadcast two hours a week to start with, then so be it. My own station now broadcasts 24/7, but we started by broadcasting one two-hour show every three weeks. Only once I had two or three other presenters on board did we go 24/7 using pre-recorded music shows when we weren't broadcasting live.

Secondly, there is the cost factor. Some server providers (see "Servers" chapter) offer a "pay-as-you-go" service where you pay in advance for a certain number of gigabytes of server usage, whereas other providers ask you to pay a flat fee per month. With the pay-as-you-go option, the bytes/gigabytes are gradually used up each time you broadcast. The amount of gigabytes used during any one broadcast will depend on both the number of listeners you have and the sound quality (and therefore the number of kilobytes per second) that you broadcast at. For example, my own radio station broadcasts live commentaries of football matches involving small semi-professional football clubs. For those broadcasts we get anything between 30 and 200 simultaneous listeners, although it is usually at the lower to middle region of those figures. This costs us approximately £20 of gigabytes every couple of months if we broadcast in stereo CD quality sound at 128 kilobytes per second (kbps). Whereas a similar radio station I know at a professional football club broadcasts a chat show two hours a week. But they get around 600 listeners each week and can't afford to broadcast at 128kbps, so they broadcast at 40kbps which uses less bytes in their two-hour show. For them, this is fine because they are only broadcasting speech. If they were to also broadcast music like us, then the sound quality at 40kbps would be poor.

Will I need licences to broadcast music?

In most countries there is a need to purchase a licence to play music recordings to the public, whether on traditional radio services, internet radio, theatre productions or ambience music in restaurants etc.

In the UK, there are two licences required. The first is from Phonographic Performance Limited (PPL) who use the licence fees to pay royalties to the performers and music rights holders of recordings in the PPL repertoire (which is most professional recordings). They offer a Small Webcaster Licence for small internet radio stations which have annual income revenue of less than £5,000. See www.ppluk.com for more information.

The other licence is from PRS for Music (The Performing Rights Society) who collect fees to pay the royalties for the writers, composers and publishers of the music. They issue a Limited Online Music Licence (LOML) where the income generated by the radio service is less than £12,500 per year.

Another licensing authority is Broadcast Music Inc. (BMI) based in the USA. www.bmi.com .

Basically, it depends which licensing organisation's repertoire the tracks you are playing come under and you can do a search of these repertoires on the organisations' respective websites.

Is there a particular type of audience I want to attract?

This is something you will need to consider before you start. The type of programmes you broadcast and their style will need to be compatible with your audience. For example, our radio station is football (soccer) related, and therefore statistically most of our listeners are males in the 25 to 40 age bracket. This won't necessarily affect the style of our commentary and magazine shows, but it does affect the style of our music shows. We therefore concentrate on playing music which is adult contemporary, with occasional oldies and current chart music thrown in. We also offer themed shows concentrating on one particular genre of music (rock, soul, 70s, 80s, 90s etc.) together with the odd show featuring comedy tracks and another featuring indie artists. By having this style policy, it will hopefully hold the interest of our listeners who will continue to tune-in and boost our listener figures.

Equipment

The amount and quality of your equipment will depend on what you want to do, and your budget. In this chapter I will take you through the basic equipment needed to get you up and running, together with additional equipment you may require for certain functions if desired. I will also share with you information about the equipment we use at our radio station in case you simply want to copy us.

Some online broadcasters, particularly those using Shoutcast servers (see "Servers" chapter) prefer to use media players on their computer, such as Winamp, to broadcast. In Winamp, broadcasters can compile a playlist of tracks (music or otherwise) to play, and there is a button on the media player plug-in to click when the presenter wants to speak. This will cause the music to "dip" so that the presenter's voice can be heard. Once the presenter has stopped speaking and un-clicked the button, the music will return to its original volume. Although this is a free and quick way to facilitate a music/speech mix function when broadcasting, it can also be a cumbersome method where the "dips" in the music can be too deep or not low enough or not very well timed, thus coming across as a bit "unprofessional". Now don't get me wrong! I'm not suggesting here that all broadcasts need to sound professional. After all, most of us online broadcasters are not professional, and it may be that using the Winamp media player as a mixer/console is fine for your needs. But if you are looking for your station's sound to appear more professional, then I suggest you may wish to consider purchasing an audio mixer. Mixers allow you to "mix" music, speech, advertisements and jingles together by assigning a separate "channel" for each piece of sound-making equipment (microphone 1, microphone 2, mp3 player, radio microphone etc.). Mixers will therefore vary in size depending on how many pieces of sound making equipment you are running through them. As each piece of equipment has its own fader (or channel), you can decide which pieces of equipment to be used together or separately etc. On my radio station we use a Behringer XENYX1204 mixer (see Fig.1) which I purchased from a live music supplies shop in central London for £126.00 in 2008. This mixer has 4 microphone channels and two stereo audio input channels. We use three of the microphone channels for our live commentaries. Two of the microphones are for the commentators, and another microphone is to pick up the atmosphere in the stadium. We use one of the stereo audio input channels to play adverts/station identity jingles (idents) and pre-recorded interviews through my mp3 player. Similarly, we will often use all 4 microphone channels if we are broadcasting an in-studio chat/discussion show or covering a football supporters' public meeting. If you are thinking of broadcasting music shows, you may decide that you want more than two audio channels and only say 2 microphone channels.

The microphones we use for in-studio broadcasts are Pro-Sound YU-37 Dynamic Microphones (see Fig. 4) which you can purchase from large electronic supplies stores. You may also require a number of microphone desk stands or floor stands depending on what you want to do. For our commentaries I decided to buy two Beyer Dynamic D109 headphones. These are headphones which have a microphone boom attached on the side. The sound quality is very good from these microphones. I have also purchased two radio microphones which are useful for outside broadcast interviews. As with anything in this field of electronics, you tend to get what you pay for. Our radio microphones were quite cheap, the sound is OK, but as soon as the user turns their back on the radio receiver base unit, the signal is lost.

Of course, if you're going to broadcast on the internet, you need some kind of computer. You can use your home PC. We tend to attach our audio mixer to our laptop using a lead from the left/right main audio output sockets on back of the mixer to the 35mm stereo minijack microphone socket on the laptop (usually found near the headphone socket). Whether this works on your computer may largely depend on whether your sound card allows it. You may also need to adjust the sound card recording level settings in your computer's control panel as sometimes they are set to "0" as a default.

If you are going to broadcast away from your studio you may wish to consider purchasing a mobile broadband dongle (see Fig 8). These are available from most mobile phone service providers but at time of going to press they do tend to vary with their coverage areas. Some service providers have a much better coverage area than others and you may wish to shop around by looking at the respective coverage areas on the various service provider websites.

Servers

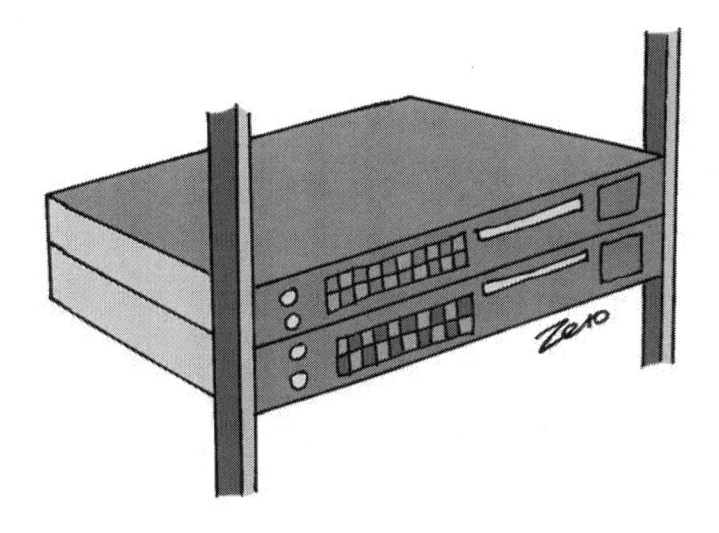

When I was first looking at setting up my radio station, I found out that there are two ways of broadcasting using a server. Firstly by creating and running a broadcast server yourself (which is free of charge), secondly by paying a server provider (or "server host") to create and run a server for you, which you would login to whenever you wanted to broadcast. I tried to set up the first option (being the cheaper one!). I followed quite detailed instructions which I found on the internet to setup the server, but then received some advice which made me change my mind.

If you broadcast using your own created server, then the only way people can tune-in to it is if they know your Internet Protocol (IP) address. Without wanting to get too technical, an IP address is a unique sequence of numbers which everyone who uses the internet will have when they are connected. If others know your IP address then there is an increased risk that your computer could be "hacked" into using the internet. Having eliminated this choice, I was left with the safest option which was to pay a server host. This turned out to be the best option because the server host does all the hard technical work for you and of course it also eliminates the risk of hackers.

Server hosts, it seems, come in two types. Those who request a set payment up front for broadband use over a specific period, and those who offer a pay-as-you-go service where you still pay in advance, but your balance is only reduced as people listen, by the amount of internet bandwidth you've actually used. How much bandwidth you use on the pay-as-you-go option will depend on:

1) the sound quality or number of kilobytes per second (kbps) that you broadcast at; and,
2) the number of simultaneous listeners that you get.

The higher the sound quality, the more bandwidth you will use per listener. Therefore the higher the sound quality, and the more simultaneous listeners you have, the faster your credit will be used up. Equally, if you have no listeners at all, none of your credit will be used up. At our radio station we don't get that many listeners (about 2000 in any 30 days at the most) and so for most of the time we find we can afford to broadcast in CD quality stereo sound (128kbps). Affordability may therefore be a factor in deciding the quality of sound you want to use.

There are a number of server providers out there, but we recommend Internet Radio at http://servers.internet-radio.com who are based in the UK. We have used them since 2008 and we have found their servers to be extremely reliable. They also offer a pay-as-you-go service which is ideal for the broadcaster with a smaller audience/budget. Once you have signed up and they have created your server, you will get access to an online control panel where you can manage your server, look at live and historical listener and other stats and upload pre-recorded shows to their optional "Auto DJ" service. You also receive full instructions on how to get on air and manage your server. Internet Radio has also set up a very useful network forum for their broadcasters to seek advice or share their experiences.

Imaging – sounding and looking professional

Once again, there is no need to sound or look professional and I'm not going to spend too much time on this topic. But if you are planning to generate revenue through advertising, having a "professional" image can help enormously. There are some simple practical things which you can do to achieve this.

For example:

- using your sound level meters to

conduct a sound level (volume) check for all microphones and music players before you start your broadcast, to make sure they are all "peaking" at the same sound level;
- getting a package of station jingles/advertisements recorded (see "Recommended resources" at the end of this book);
- broadcasting at the times you say you are going to and sticking to them.
- creating a website to publicise your broadcasts and programme schedule, and provide links for listeners to "tune-in";

Rigging for live broadcast

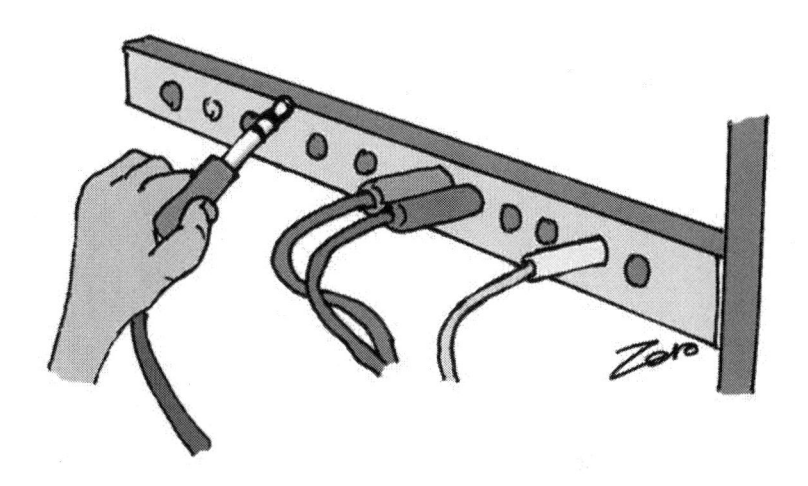

For the purposes of these instructions I will assume that you are using the following equipment:

- a Behringer XENYX1204 mixer (see Fig. 1);
- a PC or laptop with a 35mm stereo mini jack microphone socket ;
- Winamp media player on your computer to broadcast using the Shoutcast DSP Plug-in (installed separately and downloadable from www.shoutcast.com)
- Microphones (see Fig. 4) with XLR connectors linked to the Behringer audio mixer by XLR cables (see Fig 5);
- an MP3 player (or two) of some description with

a 35mm stereo minijack earphone socket. Place the mixer and computer/laptop on your table top side by side. Place the MP3 player on the table between the mixer and the laptop. Use an extension lead if required for power supply.

Plug the mixer power cable (see Fig. 2) into a power socket and the other end into the rear of the mixer.

Plug the computer/laptop power cable into another power socket and the other end into the laptop.

Start-up (boot-up) the laptop until fully ready and the desktop screen is displayed. While the laptop is starting-up, get the required number of microphones (See Fig. 4) from your bag.

Connect an XLR microphone cable (see Fig. 5) to one of the microphones and the other end into the Channel 1 female XLR three-pin input socket on top left of the mixer. This will be the main presenter's microphone. You may also choose to use some microphone desk stands if you are in your "studio".

If you want to use two microphones you can connect another XLR microphone cable to another microphone and the other end to the Channel 2 three-pin XLR input socket on top left of the mixer.

If you require an ambience (atmosphere) microphone, use a third microphone and connect it to the mixer in the same way as above, but using the Channel 3 XLR three-pin input socket.

Next you will need to connect the mixer output to the laptop so that you can send your broadcast to the internet. Use a phono lead (see Fig. 6) with two XLR adapters (see Fig. 7) on the red and white ends of the cable and a 3.5mm stereo mini-jack plug on the other end.

Connect the XLR adaptor end of the cable to the left and right main output sockets on the back of the mixer. Connect the red and white plugs on the phono cable to the XLR adaptors (it doesn't matter which coloured connector attaches to which adaptor), and attach the other end of the cable (mini-jack plug) to the microphone input socket on your computer/laptop. Shortly after doing this a window may appear on your computer/laptop screen asking you to state what type of input you have connected. If so, select "Line-in" then click OK.

Next you will need a cable with two mono quarter-inch jack plugs on one end, and a 3.5mm mini-jack plug on the other (see Fig. 9). This lead is used to connect the earphone socket on your MP3 player to one of the two quarter-inch input sockets on an audio channel on your mixer.

All the hardware is now practically set-up – all you need to do now is turn on the mixer. The power switch can be found at the back of the mixer next to the power lead. Please note that there are two power switches at the back of this particular mixer (DO NOT SWITCH ON THE "PHANTOM" POWER SWITCH BY MISTAKE – ONLY TURN ON THE MAIN POWER SWITCH NEAREST TO THE POWER LEAD).

Now you need to set up the internet connection on your computer/laptop. Once this is done, click on the Winamp start-up icon from your computer's desktop. Two windows will appear. All you are interested in at this point is the grey "Nullsoft SHOUTcast Source" window. Click on the "Output" tab and then click on the "Encoder" tab. Under "Encoder type" click on the drop-down menu and select "MP3 Encoder". Under "Encoder Settings", click on the drop-down menu and select one of the following, depending on the internet connection you have:

For fast internet connections using an Ethernet cable or Wi-Fi select: "128kbps 44,100 kHz stereo" for CD-quailty sound (if you can afford to broadcast at that higher quality sound – see earlier "Servers" section)

If you're using a mobile broadband dongle (see Fig. 8) to connect to the internet, I have found that the maximum broadcast speed you can use before listeners experience connection problems (or "buffering") is "56kbps 44,100 kHz mono" so use this setting as a maximum if you're using a mobile broadband dongle.

Next, still under the "Output" tab, click on the "Connection" tab. You need to type in a number of items here.

Firstly, in the "Port" box you need to type in the number of the port relating to your server. Your server host should provide you with this number once they have set up your server. They will also give you a password which should also be entered in the relevant space under the "Connection" tab.

Under "Address" you need to enter the website address of your server – this, too will be provided by your server host. Next you need to click on the "Yellow pages" tab. This is where you type in details of your broadcast. It is this information which will be displayed in your listeners' media players on their computers while they are listening. First of all the "Make this server public (Recommended)" check box needs to have a tick in it. Click on the check box if there isn't already a tick in the box. Secondly, in the box below the word "Name" enter details of your broadcast e.g. "The Golden Oldies Show with Rick O'Shea". Finally, using the drop-down menu in the "Genre" box, enter details of the type of show or type of music in your show e.g. "Soul" or "Sport" or something similar. At the foot of the "Yellow Pages" tab, you will see another check box "Send next track titles to the server (if available)", and two blank rectangular boxes, one labelled "Now", the other labelled "Next". The "Next" box is usually not accessible, but the "Now" box is where you can enter revised details of your live show while it is being broadcast and then click on "Send Update". For example, we use this to enter the latest score during live football commentaries. The latest score will then appear as text on the listeners' media players.

Next you need to connect the headphones to the mixer headphone socket. If you have two presenters doing one show, for example doing a live commentary, you can obtain a double socket adaptor (see Fig. 3) from electrical/audio supplies retailer so that two pairs of headphones can use the same socket.

YOU SHOULD NOW BE SET UP AND READY TO BROADCAST!

Starting a live broadcast

This guide assumes that you have already set-up the equipment ready for broadcast as described in the previous chapter. If you have not set-up the equipment yet, follow the instructions in the previous "Rigging for live broadcast" section.

This guide also assumes that you know how to connect your computer to the internet, and that you have the appropriate software on your laptop in order to connect to the internet via a mobile broadband dongle if one is required.

In order to start your broadcast, do the following:

Connect to the internet either by plugging a broadband Ethernet cable into the back of the laptop, logging on to a Wi-Fi connection, or by inserting a mobile broadband dongle into one of the USB ports on the laptop.

Once connected to the internet, make sure all the sliding faders on the mixer are in the off (down) position (towards you).

Connecting your broadcast to the internet

Having already configured the Nullsoft SHOUTcast Source window (as per instructions in the "Rigging for a live broadcast" section), on your computer/laptop click on the "Output" tab in the same window, then click on the "Connect" button to start broadcasting. You can tell if you're broadcasting because the number of bytes you are using will be ticking over in the "status" box. Listeners should now be able to "tune-in" to your broadcast but will not hear anything until you "open" the sliding faders for your microphones or the mp3 player.

Using the mixer during broadcast

Firstly, ensure the grey "master" faders on the right side of the mixer are slightly "open" (away from you about 1 or 2 notches). These control the master volume levels for all the other fader channels.

Your listeners will only be able to hear things from your mixer when the relevant sliding faders are in the "open" position (away from you). The sliding faders have the same function as any volume control on home audio equipment, it's just that instead of turning the volume control up and down, you are sliding it up and down. The further away from you that you slide the fader, the louder the output will be from that source. There will be one fader per microphone and one fader for the mp3 player. Use the mp3 player to play music tracks, jingles, adverts, recorded interviews and other features.

Monitoring your listeners

If your server is hosted by Internet Radio in the UK, you can monitor the number of listeners you have at any one time at http://uk3.internet-radio.com/client/index.php (no www needed in the address). The user name and password is the one sent to you by Internet Radio when you sign up with them. Other server hosts may have different methods for managing your server.

Please note that it is not recommended that you open your internet browser whilst broadcasting using a mobile broadband dongle, because this may slow the speed of your internet connection for the broadcast and listeners may get an interrupted service.

Recording a broadcast

To record the broadcast as an MP3 file for archiving or repeat broadcast, use audio editing software such as Audacity which is free to download. Simply open the Audacity program then click on the record button which is round and grey with a red disc in the centre. Leave the Audacity recording running for the length of the broadcast.

After the broadcast has ended, don't forget to stop the recording and save the recording in Audacity. You may wish to edit the Audacity recording at this point (or later) in order to tidy-up the beginning and end of the recorded broadcast. To do this, scroll back to the beginning of the recording and click your cursor just before the first legitimate sound has been recorded. A thin black line will appear on the screen. Next, place your cursor over this line and the cursor will change into a pointing hand. When this happens, click and hold down the left mouse button and drag the cursor to the left and as far left as you can go. This will highlight the recorded silence you have at the beginning of the recording. Once this silence has been highlighted to just before the proper broadcast begins, click on "edit" at the top of the screen, then click on "remove audio", then "cut". The silence will then disappear from the beginning of the recording.

Repeat the same process for any silence at the end of the recording.

Next you will need to convert your recording into an MP3 file. To do this click on "File", then "Export....". A new window will open asking you where on your computer/laptop you want to save the mp3 file when it is created, and what you want to call it (file name). Whichever name you choose, it must end with the suffix ".mp3". Next, you need to ensure that you are saving the file at the correct bit rate. To do this click on "Options" then choose the required bit rate of the MP3 file. Once you have entered the file name, click on

"Save". A smaller window headed "Edit the ID3 tags for the mp3 file" will now appear. This is where you can enter show information which will be displayed in the listeners' media players if the show is going to be re-broadcast. Simply fill in the show details, remembering that the "Artist" field displays first in the media players. Then click on "OK". Audacity will now convert the file to an MP3 file and store it at the location you chose. This conversion may take up to 15 or 20 minutes to finish depending on the length of the recording, so why not pack away while this happens.

Pre-recorded shows

There is no reason why you can't pre-record shows for broadcast, particularly music shows. The Internet Radio company (see "Servers" section) also offers an Auto DJ service where you can either upload individual song tracks/jingles/adverts or complete shows in MP3 format to the Auto DJ server. The MP3 files will then be broadcast in rotation infinitum until you de-activate the Auto DJ (e.g. in order to broadcast a live show).

We use the Audacity software (see previous section) to pre-record and edit music shows which we broadcast in rotation whenever we're not broadcasting live. If you usually use the microphone socket on your computer to link your audio mixer to your computer for broadcasting, then you will be able to do the same for recording shows. In fact, you don't even necessarily need an audio mixer, although you are more likely to be able to mix your sounds better with one. You will also need a mixer if you are going to speak between tracks. If you're simply recording a continuous music show without speech, then you could record it without using a mixer. You could simply connect your MP3 player to your computer using a male 35mm stereo minijack plug to male 35mm stereo minijack plug lead (see Fig.10).

If you are recording a music show but don't have the PRS or PPL licences, you can always play royalty-free music, or music recorded by "unsigned" acts. There are a number of websites you can obtain this music from such as www.rradiomusic.com , who have put together some 20-minute shows of new music in a variety of music genres from the USA and around the World.

Fig 1 - A Behringer XENYX1204 audio mixer

Fig 2 - The mixer power lead

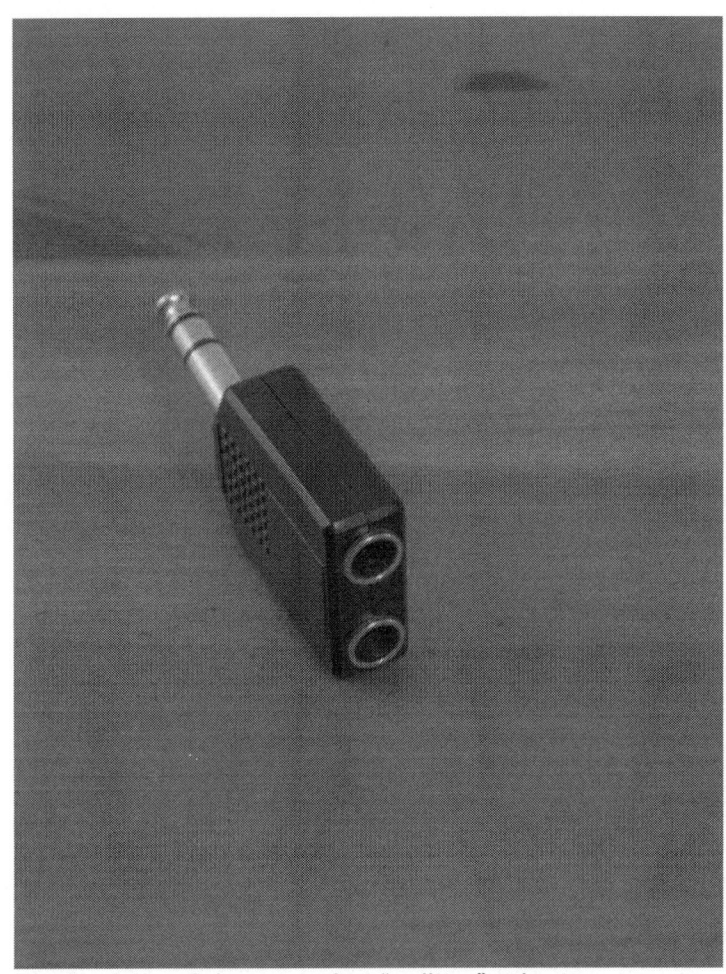

Fig 3 - A headphone socket "splitter" adaptor

Fig 4 - A Pro-Sound YU-37 dynamic microphone

Fig 5 - An XLR cable and male/female connectors

Fig 6 - A phono to 3.5mm minijack lead

Fig 7 - Two XLR (female) to phono (female) adaptors

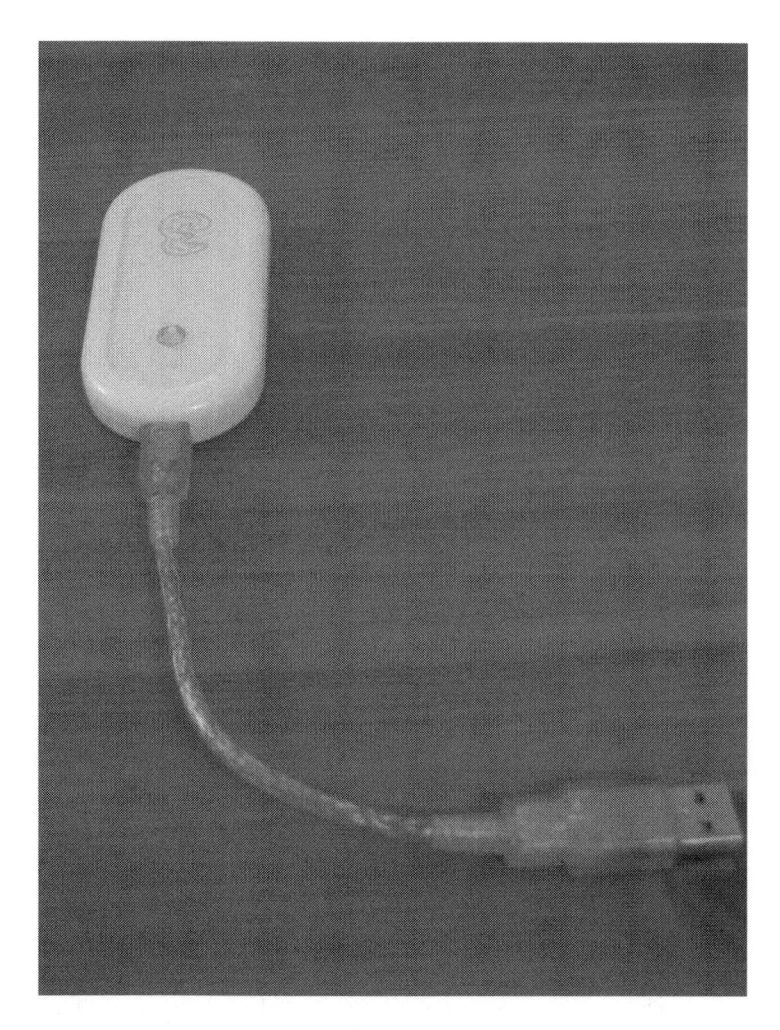

Fig 8 - A mobile broadband "dongle"

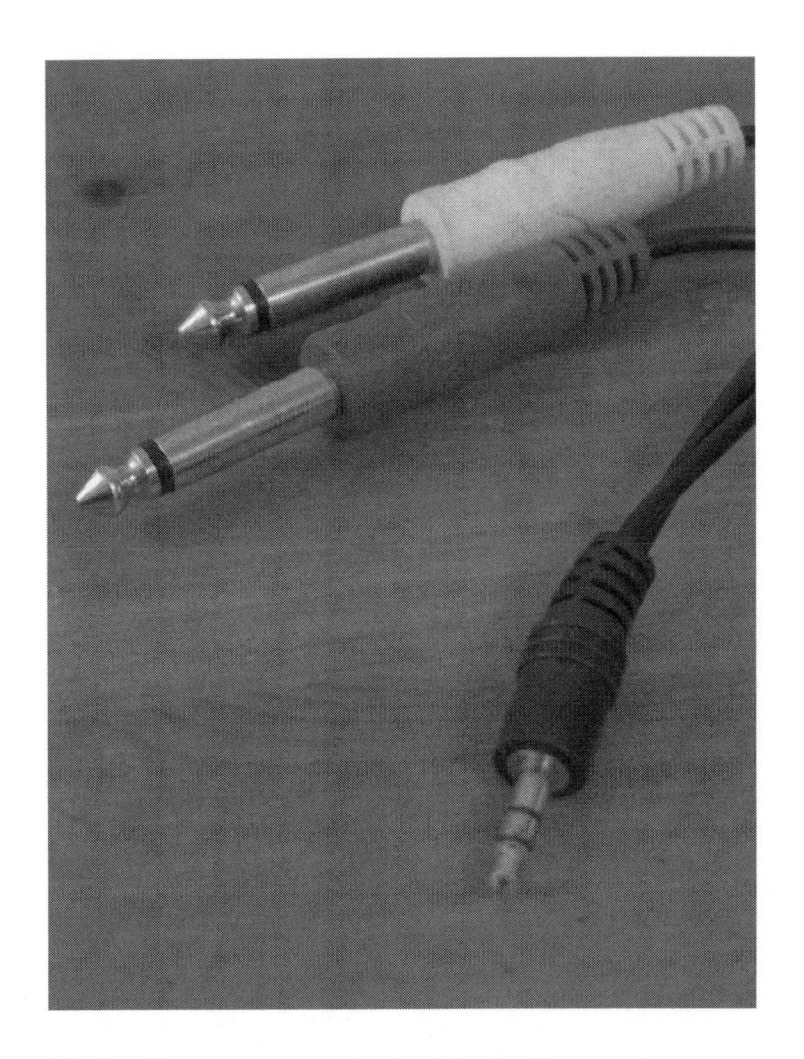

Fig 9 - Two mono quarter-inch jacks to one stereo minijack lead

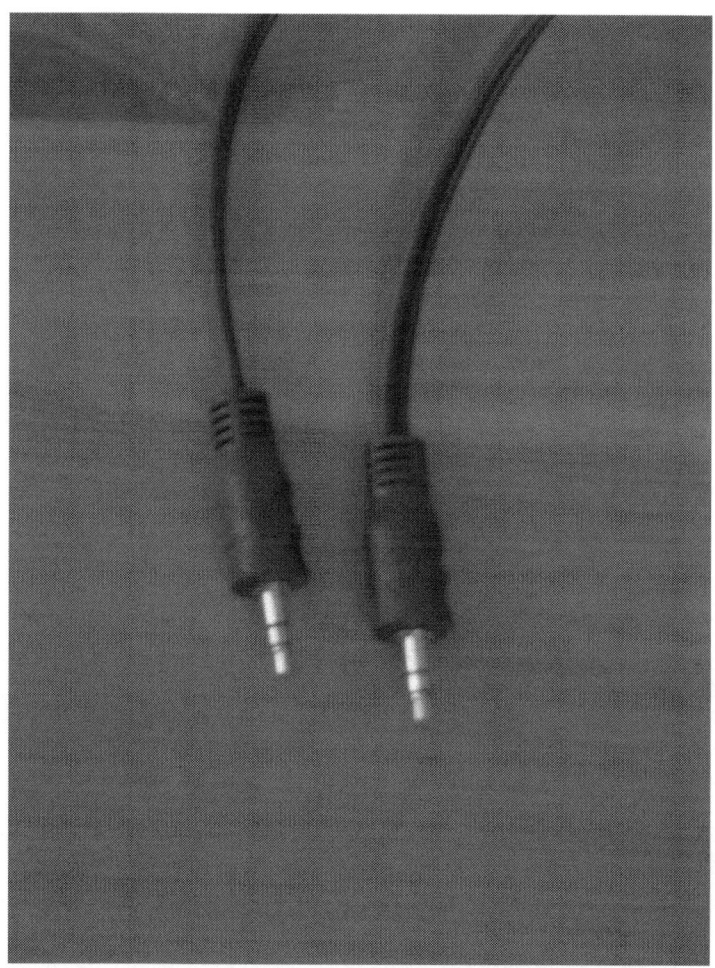

Fig 10 - A stereo minijack to stereo minijack lead

Recommended resources (UK)

High quality and inexpensive jingles/adverts etc.:

http://stoneslive.co.uk/id12.html

07821 719818

Broadcast server hosting:

Internet Radio: http://servers.internet-radio.com/

Mobile broadband:

www.three.co.uk

Audio recording software:

Audacity

Download from: http://audacity.sourceforge.net

Website design and hosting:

Furst Web Design: http://www.furst.co.uk/index.htm

07905 357140

Printed in Great Britain
by Amazon